# Body Fuel for Healthy Bodies
## Grains, Bread, Cereal, and Pasta

Trisha Sertori

**Marshall Cavendish**
Benchmark

New York

First published in 2008 by
macmillan education australia pty ltd
15–19 Claremont Street, South Yarra 3141

Visit our website at www.macmillan.com.au or go directly to www.macmillanlibrary.com.au

Associated companies and representatives throughout the world.

Library of Congress Cataloging-in-Publication Data

Sertori, Trisha.
  Grains, bread, cereal, and pasta / by Trisha Sertori.
    p. cm. — (Body fuel for healthy bodies)
  Includes index.
  ISBN 978-0-7614-3800-7
  1. Nutrition—Juvenile literature. 2. Food crops—Juvenile literature.  I. Title.
  TX355.S422 2008
  613.2—dc22

                                            2008026206


Edited by Margaret Maher
Text and cover design by Stella Vassiliou
Page layout by Stella Vassiliou
Photo research by Claire Francis
Illustrations by Toby Quarmby, Vishus Productions, pp. 4, 5; Jeff Lang and
  Stella Vassiliou, pp. 8, 9 (below); all others by Stella Vassiliou.

Printed in the United States

**Acknowledgments**
The author and publishers are grateful to the following for permission to reproduce copyright material:

Cover and header photos courtesy of © iStockphoto.com (assorted grains); © iStockphoto.com/Galina Barskaya (girl); © iStockphoto.com/Andres Peiro Palmer (assorted breads); © iStockphoto.com/Kristian Sekulic (boy).

Photos courtesy of:
123RF/Andrew Brown, **29** (bottom); 123RF/Kailash Soni, **7** (middle left); Artville/Burke Triolo Productions, **28** (2nd bottom); © Artman/Dreamstime.com, **29** (2nd bottom); © Peter Clark/Dreamstime.com, **6** (top); © Ryan Pike/Dreamstime.com, **12**; © Nicholas Rjabow/Dreamstime.com, **29** (top); Getty Images/Colin Cooke, **25**; Getty Images/Andy Crawford, **7** (top left); Getty Images/George Doyle, **18** (top); Getty Images/Jack Hollingsworth, **23** (bottom); Getty Images/Becky Reed, **23** (middle);Getty Images/ David Sutherland, **22** (right); Andersen Ross/Getty Images, **15** (bottom); Photolibrary/Tim Hill/Alamy, **17** (bottom right); © iStockphoto.com, **17** (middle right), **19**, **28** (bottom & 2nd top); © iStockphoto.com/Alexey Aleshkin, **29** (3rd top); © iStockphoto.com/Linda Alstead, **7** (bottom left); © iStockphoto.com/Elke Dennis, **22** (bottom left); © iStockphoto.com/Rebecca Ellis, **17** (top right); © iStockphoto.com/Oleg Fedorenko, **6** (bottom); © iStockphoto.com/Bill Grove, **14**; © iStockphoto.com/Jim Jurica, **20** (top right); © iStockphoto.com/Gary Milner, **11** (top); © iStockphoto.com/Dóri O'Connell. **15** (middle); © iStockphoto.com/John Peacock, **21** (top); © iStockphoto.com/Andres Peiro Palmer, **1, 3**; © iStockphoto.com/John Sigler, **22** (top); © iStockphoto.com/Maartje Van Caspel, **23** (top left); MEA Photos/Lesya Bryndzia, **28** (top); MEA Photos/Claire Francis, **26** (top); Photolibrary/Bill Bachmann/Alamy, **22** (middle left); Photolibrary/John Bavosi/Science Photo Library, **13** (right); Photolibrary/Bubbles Photolibrary/Alamy, **27**; Photolibrary/Eye of Science/Science Photo Library, **24** (bottom); Photolibrary/Foodfolio/Alamy, **16, 29** (2nd top); Photolibrary/Tim Hill/Alamy, **17** (bottom right); Photolibrary/Professors PM Motta & FM Magliocca/Science Photo Library, **24** (top); Photolibrary/Ivany Sandra, **30**; © Claudio Baldini/Shutterstock, **20** (bottom right); © Andi Berger/Shutterstock, **8, 9** (bottom), **10**; © Radu Razvan/Shutterstock, **29** (3rd bottom).

MyPyramid symbols courtesy of U.S. Department of Agriculture.

While every care has been taken to trace and acknowledge copyright, the publisher tenders their apologies for any accidental infringement where copyright has proved untraceable. Where the attempt has been unsuccessful, the publisher welcomes information that would redress the situation.

# Contents

What Is Body Fuel?                                                          **4**

What Types of Grains, Bread, Cereal, and Pasta Are There?                  **6**

The Digestive System                                                        **8**

What Nutrients Are in Grains, Bread, Cereal, and Pasta?                    **12**

Fueling the Body with Grains, Bread, Cereal, and Pasta                     **14**

Healthy Food Choices                                                       **16**

Functional Foods                                                           **18**

Naturally Healthy Grains, Bread, Cereal, and Pasta                         **20**

Grains, Bread, Cereal, and Pasta Around the World                          **22**

Allergies and Intolerances to Grains, Bread, Cereal, and Pasta             **24**

Checking Food Labels for Grains, Bread, Cereal, and Pasta                  **26**

Cooking Class                                                              **28**

   *Whole-grain Bread with Mixed Fruit*                       **28**

Fueling the Body with Healthy Grains, Bread, Cereal, and Pasta             **30**

Glossary                                                                   **31**

Index                                                                      **32**

## Glossary Words

When a word is printed in **bold**, you can look up its meaning in the Glossary on page 31.

# What Is Body Fuel?

Body fuel is the energy, vitamins, and minerals we need to live. Just as cars need gasoline and computers need electricity, people need energy, vitamins, and minerals to work.

The best way to fuel our bodies is with a **balanced diet**. A balanced diet gives us all the **nutrients** our bodies need.

## Nutrients in Foods

The nutrients in foods are divided into macronutrients and micronutrients.

Macronutrients provide energy. They are proteins, carbohydrates, and fats and oils. Micronutrients help **chemical reactions** take place in the body. They are vitamins and minerals.

## The Food Pyramid

The food pyramid lists foods for healthy bodies. The colors shown (from left to right) are for grains, vegetables, fruit, oils, dairy, and meat and beans.

MyPyramid.gov
STEPS TO A HEALTHIER YOU

**Fabulous Body Fuel Fact**

Cereals are named after the ancient Roman goddess of corn, Ceres.

# Grains, Bread, Cereal, and Pasta

Grains, bread, cereal, and pasta are foods made from seeds called grains. Grains come from different kinds of grasses, such as wheat and rice.

Grain-based foods supply slow-burning carbohydrates and **fiber** for healthy bodies.

## Staple Foods

Grain-based foods are often called staple foods. This means foods that are the main part of a person's diet. Grains are easily stored and often maintain nutrient content for many years.

## The Food Pyramid

Grains, bread, cereal, and pasta are found in the orange part of the food pyramid. People need to choose most of their foods from this group every day.

### Body Fuel Health Tips

Grain-based foods are the main food for most humans. In some countries, cereals supply most of the energy and protein in people's diets. In Western countries, carbohydrates supply 25 to 50 percent of people's energy and protein.

## Grain Group
Make half your grains whole

MyPyramid.gov

# What Types Of Grains, Bread, Cereal, and Pasta Are There?

Grains are the base ingredient of bread, cereal, and pasta. People all over the world depend on grains as a major source of carbohydrates.

### Grains
Grains originally came from wild grasses, such as wheat, corn, millet, and oats. People began farming these grasses for food thousands of years ago.

### Bread
Bread is commonly made from wheat, millet, or corn. It is eaten in almost every country. In Australia, Europe, and the United States, most breads are cooked with **yeast**. In other places, such as Africa and India, bread is cooked without yeast. These breads are flat, like a pancake.

## Fabulous Body Fuel Fact

Corn is one of the largest grasses in the world. This means corn seeds are grains, not vegetables. Ears of corn are like giant ears of wheat or rice.

## Fabulous Body Fuel Fact

Pasta was first made in China. During the thirteenth century, the Italian explorer Marco Polo traveled to China and took the pasta recipe back to Italy. Italy is now famous for its pasta.

### Cereals

Cereals are made from lots of different grains. These grains are **milled**, rolled, or steamed so they are soft enough to eat. Most cereals come from oats, wheat, rice, or corn.

### Rice

Rice is a carbohydrate source for more than half of the world's population. There are many different kinds of rice. Each has different vitamins and minerals, but they all have a similar amount of carbohydrate. Rice is eaten as a boiled grain, or made into porridge or rice noodles.

### Pasta

Pasta is usually made from wheat called semolina or durum wheat. The wheat is ground into flour and mixed into a dough with water. Spaghetti and other pastas are made by spinning or rolling the dough.

## Body Fuel Health Tips

Carbohydrates can be long, medium, or short. Long carbohydrates, like fiber, are hardest to digest. Fiber might only be partly digested or not digested at all. Medium, short, or "single" carbohydrates, such as sucrose, lactose, and glucose, are completely digested and used for energy.

# The Digestive System

The digestive system breaks down the foods we eat so they are ready to be absorbed into the bloodstream. Each part of the digestive system plays a part in breaking down, or digesting, foods. **Saliva** and **digestive enzymes** prepare to digest foods even before we eat them. They are produced when we see or smell foods.

### Mouth
Teeth cut and grind food into smaller pieces. The enzymes in saliva start to break down carbohydrates in the food. The chewed food becomes a **bolus**, which is pushed down the throat by the tongue when we swallow.

### Liver
The liver filters nutrients from the blood. Nutrients are sent to the small intestine for digestion. Waste is sent to the large intestine.

### Gallbladder
The gallbladder stores bile, which is a digestive liquid made by the liver. Bile is used in the small intestine to break down fats.

### Small Intestine
The small intestine is almost 23 feet (7 meters) long. Foods are digested in the small intestine after they are broken down in the stomach. Most nutrients are absorbed into our bloodstream through **villi** in the small intestine.

### Esophagus
The bolus travels down the esophagus (ee-*soff*-a-gus) to the stomach.

### Stomach
Stomach muscles churn the bolus. Acid in the stomach makes the food watery.

### Pancreas
The pancreas makes enzymes that break down macronutrients.

### Large Intestine
The large intestine is 5 feet (1.5 meters) long. It carries waste to the **rectum** for **evacuation** as **feces** (*fee*-seas).

## Fabulous Body Fuel Fact

A bolus takes about three seconds to reach your stomach after it is swallowed.

# How Does the Body Digest Grains, Bread, Cereal, and Pasta?

Grain-based foods are rich in carbohydrates. The body makes an enzyme called amylase (*am*-ill-ays) to break down carbohydrates into glucose. Glucose is a simple sugar that is easily converted to energy.

## The Mouth

Carbohydrate digestion starts in the mouth. Saliva contains amylase to break down carbohydrates while food is chewed.

## The Stomach

When the bolus reaches the stomach it becomes more watery. Stomach muscles churn the food mixture so it becomes like watery soup.

## Pancreas and Small Intestine Working Together

The partly digested food then travels to the small intestine. This is where final digestion occurs. The pancreas makes more amylase and sends it to the small intestine. The last of the carbohydrate is broken down into glucose for absorption in the small intestine.

## Large Intestine

Waste travels to the large intestine, where some is **fermented** by bacteria. This releases any remaining nutrients. The waste that is not digested is evacuated as feces.

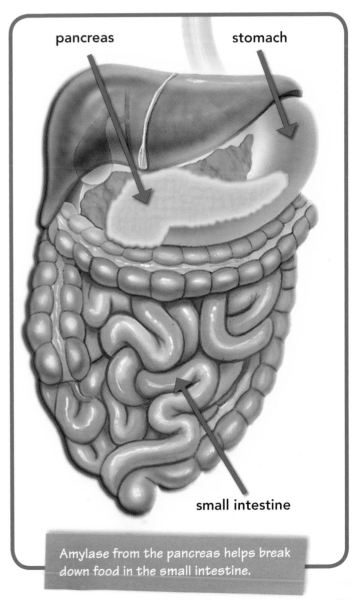

pancreas

stomach

small intestine

Amylase from the pancreas helps break down food in the small intestine.

# How Does the Digestive System Absorb Grains, Bread, Cereal, and Pasta?

The digestive system breaks down carbohydrates from grains, bread, cereals, rice, and pasta into glucose. Glucose is absorbed into the bloodstream through villi on the walls of the small intestine. Blood transports the glucose throughout the body to be used for energy.

## Insulin

As glucose enters the bloodstream, the pancreas makes a special **hormone** called insulin. Insulin measures and controls how much blood sugar is available to be used for body fuel. The bloodstream carries absorbed glucose, insulin, and nutrients to **cells** throughout the body.

## Metabolism

The chemical reactions in cells that convert nutrients into energy are called metabolism. As the body absorbs nutrients, they are metabolized into energy. Body tissue is built from the energy. Metabolism occurs in every living thing, every second of the day.

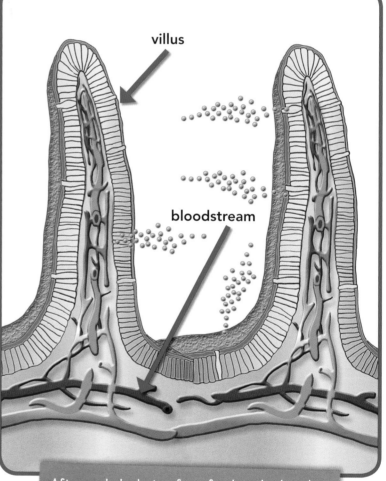

After carbohydrates from food are broken down they enter the bloodstream as glucose.

## Fabulous Body Fuel Fact

Bread and rice are so important that bread is sometimes called "the staff of life" and Hindus pray to the goddess of Rice, called Sri.

# How Do Grains, Bread, Cereal, and Pasta Help the Body Function?

Grains, bread, cereal, and pasta provide energy for the body in the form of glucose. When glucose enters cells, chemical reactions change it to energy, or body fuel. This body fuel can be made from all the macronutrients. Carbohydrates provide efficient energy because they can be changed into energy quickly.

## Insulin

Insulin keeps the level of glucose in the blood stable. The body stabilizes blood glucose levels because too much or too little can make people sick.

As digested carbohydrates enter the bloodstream, the amount of glucose in the blood rises. When this happens, insulin tells cells to absorb the glucose and convert it to energy. This brings blood glucose levels back to normal.

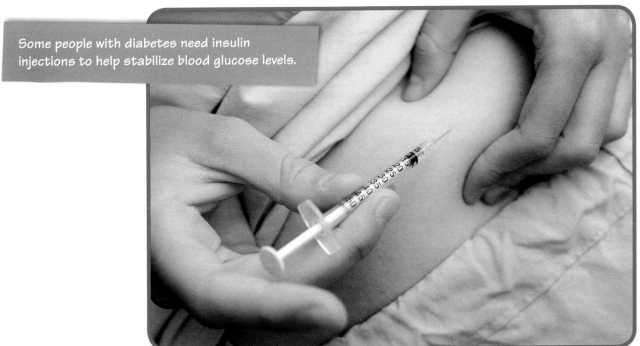

Some people with diabetes need insulin injections to help stabilize blood glucose levels.

## Body Fuel Health Tips

Most people can change glucose to energy after thirty minutes. However, if someone has **diabetes** it takes longer for the body to remove glucose from the blood.

# What Nutrients Are in Grains, Bread, Cereal, and Pasta?

Carbohydrates are the most important nutrient in grains, bread, cereal, and pasta. These foods also have minerals, essential fatty acids, vitamins, and **phytochemicals** (*fie*-toe-chemicals).

Grains, breads, cereals, rice, and pasta have a range of micronutrients and high levels of fiber.

| Nutrients in Grains, Bread, Cereal, and Pasta | | | | | |
|---|---|---|---|---|---|
| **Nutrients** | **Grains** | **Bread** | **Cereal** | **Brown Rice** | **Pasta** |
| **Macronutrients** | | | | | |
| carbohydrate | • | • | • | • | • |
| protein | • | • | • | • | • |
| fats and oils | • | • | • | | • |
| **Micronutrients** | | | | | |
| **Vitamins** | | | | | |
| vitamin B1 | • | • | • | • | • |
| vitamin B2 | • | • | • | • | • |
| vitamin B3 | • | • | • | • | • |
| vitamin E | | | | • | |
| **Minerals** | | | | | |
| iron | • | • | • | • | • |
| magnesium | | | • | • | |
| phosphorous | • | | | | |
| potassium | • | | • | | |
| zinc | | | • | • | |
| **Fatty acids** | | | | | |
| omega-3 fatty acid | • | | | | |

Different grain-based foods provide different micronutrients.

# How Does the Body Use These Nutrients?

The body uses carbohydrates from grains, breads, cereals, rice, and pasta to produce energy. Other nutrients in grains, such as vitamins and minerals, are used throughout the body. However, the quality of these nutrients in grain foods is low compared to other foods, such as meat.

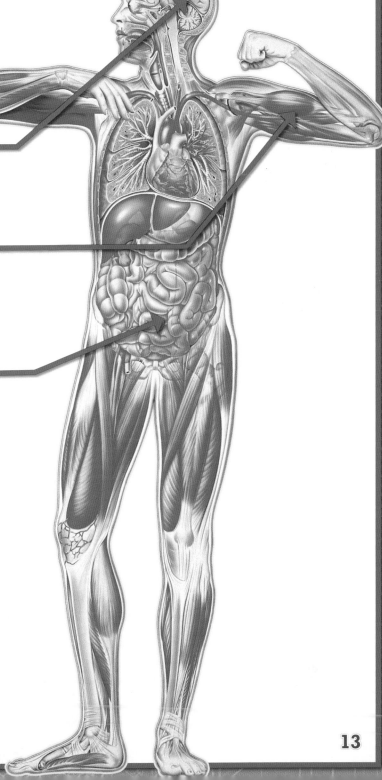

**Brain**
Minerals and B-group vitamins in grain foods assist healthy brain function. Carbohydrates fuel the brain with energy.

**Muscles**
The muscles in the body use energy from carbohydrates to function.

**Large Intestine**
The fiber in grain-based foods helps remove waste from the body.

## Body Fuel Health Tips

Bacteria ferment undigested carbohydrates in the large intestine, producing fatty acids and gas. The body uses the fatty acids for energy and stores them in the liver. They may help protect the digestive system against cancer.

# Fueling the Body with Grains, Bread, Cereal, and Pasta

Carbohydrates are the main body fuel in grains, bread, cereal, and pasta. Carbohydrates have 3.8 **calories** (sixteen kilojoules) of energy per gram. Adolescent boys age ten to twelve doing moderate exercise need about 1,800 to 2,200 cal (7,500–9,500 kJ) of energy daily. Girls the same age need a bit less, about 1,800 to 2,000 cal (7,500 –8,500 kJ). Almost half of these calories are needed just to keep us alive.

## Burning Energy

Daily activities burn differing amounts of energy. A 77-pound (35-kilogram) child watching television burns approximately 42 cal (174 kJ) per hour. Running burns approximately 403 cal (1,688 kJ) per hour, and fast walking burns approximately 167 cal (698 kJ) per hour. Cleaning up your bedroom burns approximately 134 cal (560 kJ) per hour.

## Daily Activities

Most of our daily calories should come from grain-based foods, such as cereals, rice, and bread. This is because glucose energy from carbohydrates is the most efficient body fuel.

Joining in a race can be fun—and it burns more than 400 calories per hour!

# The Glycemic Index

The glycemic index (gly-*see*-mick index) (G.I.) shows how quickly foods raise blood glucose levels. A high G.I. means a food raises glucose levels rapidly. Healthy carbohydrate energy is food with a low G.I. This food releases glucose into the bloodstream slowly.

## Choose Low-G.I.

People need to choose low-G.I., high-fiber carbohydrates at every meal. This supplies the slow, sustained release of energy we need to function throughout the day. People need at least 4-1/2 oz (130 g) of low-G.I. carbohydrate foods each day.

The glycemic index ranks carbohydrates as either low, medium, or high.

- Low G.I. is fifty-five or less and is best for healthy energy.
- Medium G.I. is fifty-six to sixty-nine and is good for energy.
- High G.I. is seventy or more and is not very healthy. High G.I. foods are often sugary foods.

Low-G.I. foods, such as oats, supply lots of long-lasting energy.

People need energy from carbohydrates for all their daily activities, such as walking to school.

# Healthy Food Choices

Choosing whole-grain bread, cereals, rice, and pasta supplies vitamins, minerals, and long-lasting energy. This is because whole grains contain the **bran**, **germ**, and **endosperm** of the grain kernel. These are rich in vitamins and proteins.

## Food Preparation

The way people prepare foods can make them more healthy or less healthy. Added fats can make grain foods less healthy.

The following table shows some healthy ways to prepare and eat grain foods.

| ✓ Healthy Choices | ✗ Less Healthy Choices |
| --- | --- |
| **Breads** | |
| olive oil to replace butter | added saturated fats, such as butter or saturated margarine |
| whole-grain bread | white bread |
| white bread mixed with whole grains | |
| **Cereals** | |
| low-G.I. whole-grain cereals, such as oatmeal | high-G.I .cereals with lots of added sugar |
| **Rice** | |
| brown rice | white rice |
| boiled or steamed rice | fried rice |
| **Pasta** | |
| whole-grain pasta | pasta made from white flour |
| pasta with olive oil, seafood, and tomatoes | added saturated fats, such as butter |
| | canned spaghetti |

## Fabulous Body Fuel Fact

The body renews 6 billion cells every hour!

A healthy breakfast of whole-grain cereal helps provide energy throughout the day.

# Sugary Foods

The carbohydrates in many sugary foods, such as cake, have a high G.I. Foods with high G.I. numbers contain carbohydrates that are rapidly converted into glucose. Foods with low G.I. numbers contain carbohydrates that are slowly converted into glucose. This provides longer-lasting energy. Low-G.I. foods are a healthier choice.

## Refined Carbohydrates

Refined carbohydrates are grains that have been processed. This means most of the bran and some of the germ is removed. Grains are refined to make them better for baking or to improve the food's appearance. However, refined grains lose vitamins, minerals, protein, and fiber. Some refined grain foods are:

- sugary cereals
- pastries
- cookies
- cakes
- doughnuts.

These foods are usually made from processed white flour, with added sugar and fat.

Whole-grain bread is a great alternative to less healthy grain foods, such as pastries and sugary cereals.

### Body Fuel Health Tips

Bread is a good energy source. It is a low-fat food, rich in complex carbohydrates and fiber. Whole-grain and multigrain breads have more fiber, minerals, and vitamins than refined white bread.

# Functional Foods

Functional foods are foods that not only give us energy, but also improve our health. Some natural ingredients in foods can help protect our bodies against illnesses such as cancer, and can decrease the risk of high blood pressure or stroke. Functional foods can also make people feel healthier and improve blood circulation, skin, and hair.

## Antioxidants

Antioxidants are chemicals that help protect cells from damage. They are found in whole grains. Grains such as barley, wheat, oats, and brown rice have high levels of antioxidants.

Make your sandwich with whole-grain bread and add lettuce and tomato. These ingredients have antioxidants to help absorb free radicals.

## Free Radicals

Free radicals are substances that form during chemical reactions. They help chemical reactions take place in the body and help cells communicate. However, free radicals can also damage cells and the lining of blood vessels, causing disease. Antioxidants control the number of free radicals, helping to maintain healthy levels. They act like a sponge in the bloodstream, soaking up excess free radicals.

### Body Fuel Health Tips

Remember to eat the crust! Bread crusts contain healthy antioxidants.

## Choosing Natural Functional Foods

Many of the foods people eat are naturally functional foods. However, sometimes these foods are refined so their natural health benefits are lost. It is easy to choose functional grain foods. Simply select whole grains rather than refined grains. Always choose foods with no added fats and sugars.

Some functional grain foods are wheat germ, flaxseed, and whole grains.

- Wheat germ is part of the wheat kernel. It dissolves **cholesterol**, speeds evacuation of body waste, may reduce the risk of cancer, and it contains antioxidants.

- Flaxseed comes from the flax plant. It has antioxidants and mucilage fiber (*myou*-suh-lidge fiber), which helps keep glucose levels stable in the blood.

- Whole grains are rich in omega-3 fatty acids. Omega-3 fatty acids may improve eyesight, reduce cardiovascular disease, and lower the risk of cancer.

The seeds of the flax plant can be used in foods for extra health benefits.

# Naturally Healthy Grains, Bread, Cereal, and Pasta

Eating whole-grain breads, cereal, and pasta makes people naturally healthy. It reduces the risk of heart disease, diabetes, obesity, and cancer.

## Fiber for Health

Fiber is the part of plant foods that cannot be digested. The fiber in grain foods ferments in the large intestine. This allows the body to absorb the remaining nutrients from the food. Fiber then helps the body evacuate waste.

### Not Enough Fiber

Waste can sit in the intestines for long periods if people don't get enough fiber and water. This is called constipation, and can cause health problems. Eating whole-grain foods and drinking six glasses of water daily helps prevent constipation.

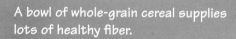

A bowl of whole-grain cereal supplies lots of healthy fiber.

## Body Fuel Health Tips

For good health you should have 15–25 g of fiber a day. For 25 g of fiber, you could eat:

- one bowl of high-fiber cereal
- two pieces of fruit
- two slices of multi-grain bread
- one cup of vegetables.

It is important to drink enough water each day to prevent constipation.

## Fabulous Body Fuel Fact

Soluble fiber not only helps nutrient absorption, it also soaks up cholesterol in the bloodstream.

## Grain Foods for Good Health

When people eats lots of grain foods they gain healthy energy and fiber. Eating grain-based carbohydrates, such as bread, also makes people feel full. They are less likely to overeat because soluble fiber swells in the stomach and slows digestion. This reduces hunger and allows the body to absorb more nutrients.

### Grain Foods with Other Foods

People absorb more nutrients from other foods when they eat them with grain foods. Make grain foods with lots of soluble fiber a base for meals with meat, dairy foods, and vegetables.

People can absorb plenty of nutrients from a whole-grain sandwich with lean meat, cheese, and lettuce and tomato.

### Body Fuel Health Tips

There are two types of fiber, insoluble and soluble. You need both for good health. Insoluble fiber is the hard or "woody" part of the food, such as apple skin. Soluble fiber is in the cells that give foods, such as apples, their shape. Oats, baked beans, and lentils are high in soluble fiber.

21

# Grains, Bread, Cereal, and Pasta Around the World

People around the world need to eat carbohydrate foods for healthy bodies. But people in different parts of the world depend on different grains for their carbohydrate foods.

### Scotland
Scotland is famous for oat porridge. Oats give people in very cold countries lots of high quality carbohydrate for energy. Oats are the most nutrient-rich of all grains.

### Middle East
A type of crushed wheat called bulgur is made into a salad called tabouli in the Middle East. Bulgur is made by crushing, steaming, and drying whole wheat kernels.

### South America
Corn is the staple grain in much of South America. Corn is ground and then cooked into flat bread called tortillas.

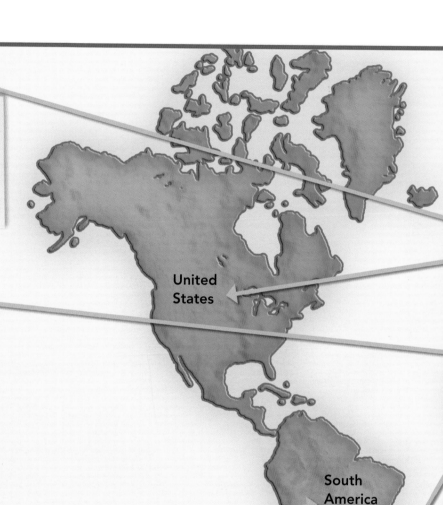

United States

South America

### Africa, India, and Eastern Europe
Millet is a staple grain in Africa and India. It is also eaten across Eastern Europe. In India, millet is made into flat breads called chapattis and rotis.

## Fabulous Body Fuel Fact

The Inca people of South America were the first people to grow corn. Today, corn is used all over the world. It is even used as fuel for engines!

As you can see from this world map, people around the world eat different amounts of the foods in the bread, cereals, rice, and pasta foods group.

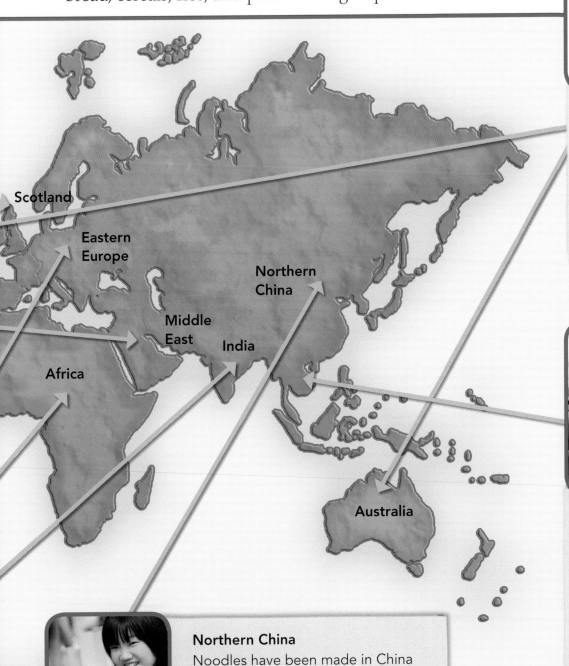

Scotland

Eastern Europe

Northern China

Middle East

India

Africa

Australia

**The United States and Australia**
Cereals and wheat or rye breads are the main grain foods eaten in the United States and Australia.

**Asia**
Millions of people across Asia depend on rice as their staple carbohydrate. Rice is eaten boiled and is also cooked as porridge or made into rice noodles.

**Northern China**
Noodles have been made in China for thousands of years. Wheat noodles are made in northern China because the climate there is ideal for growing wheat.

23

# Allergies and Intolerances to Grains, Bread, Cereal, and Pasta

Food allergies and intolerances are reactions by our bodies to different foods. A food allergy occurs when the **immune system** reacts as if a food is dangerous. This reaction may cause itchy skin or make breathing difficult. A food intolerance is a negative chemical reaction in the body to the food. These reactions often cause similar symptoms to allergic reactions.

## Common Allergies

The most common allergy to grains, breads, cereals, rice, and pasta is to gluten. Gluten is a substance formed from wheat proteins.

This allergy is called celiac (*see*-lee-ack) disease. Celiac disease affects the small intestine. It damages the villi that absorb nutrients.

### Nutrient Loss

People with untreated celiac disease may have illnesses because they cannot absorb nutrients properly. They may have **anemia** (an-*nee*-mee-a) and be deficient in many nutrients.

### Treatment

People with celiac disease heal quickly when all gluten foods are removed from their diet.

When villi are damaged by celiac disease, they are flattened and cannot absorb nutrients properly.

### Fabulous Body Fuel Fact

Gluten is the substance that makes bread dough stretchy. It allows bread to become light and fluffy.

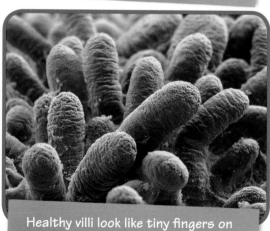

Healthy villi look like tiny fingers on the walls of the small intestine.

24

# What Can I Eat if I Am Allergic to Gluten?

People with celiac disease must completely avoid foods with gluten. Even the tiniest amount of gluten in foods causes the small intestine to become inflamed. This inflammation further damages the villi, reducing the absorption of nutrients.

## Grains with Gluten

Grains that contain gluten are rye, barley, and wheat. Some people with celiac disease also have a reaction to oats.

## Grains without Gluten

People with celiac disease can stay healthy by replacing all foods in their diet that contain gluten. Alternative grains include:

- corn
- rice
- tapioca
- millet
- sorghum
- pure buckwheat.

## Choosing Gluten-free Foods

Some gluten-free foods are:

- corn chips
- pasta made from rice
- gluten-free breads made from corn, rice, millet, or buckwheat.

Polenta, made from corn, is a popular gluten-free food.

# Checking Food Labels for Grains, Bread, Cereal, and Pasta

Food labels state all ingredients in packaged foods and their energy and nutrient levels. This information tells us if the food has preservatives and how healthy the food is.

## Nutrients

People can also compare nutrients in foods, such as cereals, by reading the food labels. Check for good levels of B-group vitamins, magnesium, potassium, and zinc. Choose cereals that are fortified with calcium and have at least 10 percent of your daily recommended fiber.

**99%**
*Real Fruit*

No Added Sugar

GLYCEMIC INDEX TESTED
G
GLYCEMIC INDEX TESTED

✔ **Low** GI Rating
✔ **No Preservatives**
✔ **No Artificial Colors**

90g NET

Food labels tell us about the ingredients found in the food.

*Body Fuel Health Tips*

Food labels state if food is gluten free. Any gluten at all is dangerous for people with celiac disease. Food labeled "gluten free" must not contain any detectable gluten, oats, or malt.

## Fabulous Body Fuel Fact

An easy way to check the nutrient levels in breads is by weight. Often the heavier the bread is the higher its nutrient content.

# Comparing Food Labels for Healthy Eating

People can improve their health by comparing ingredients on food labels. Check labels for the grains used in cereals, breads, prepared rice foods, and pastas. Choose foods that list whole grains as the first ingredient.

## Food Labels on Bread

The wheat used in bread is milled to make flour. Some wheat is lightly milled, so the bran and germ of the wheat are kept. Check food labels of the following breads:

- Whole-grain breads contain a mix of different grains. They are rich in iron, protein, B-group vitamins, minerals, and fiber.

- Wheat-flour breads have different percentages of whole-wheat grains. Some whole-wheat breads have 75 percent refined flour and just 25 percent whole grains.

- White bread contains bleached and enriched flour. White bread has the least nutrients, but helps the body absorb vitamin B1.

People can check food labels to see how much whole-grain flour is used in bread.

# Cooking Class

**Ask an adult to help you.**

Bread is one of the tastiest foods to cook at home. Follow this recipe for whole-grain bread with mixed fruit to get:

- carbohydrates for energy
- fiber for healthy digestion
- protein for cell renewal
- minerals and vitamins for healthy chemical reactions in the body.

## Whole-grain Bread with Mixed Fruit

Makes three loaves.
**Preparation time**  2 hours, including rising time
**Cooking time**  20–30 minutes

### Ingredients

2 7-gram packets dry yeast

2 tablespoons olive oil

2 tablespoons honey

2-3/4 cups of warm water

3 cups of white flour

3 cups of whole-grain flour

1/2 cup of sunflower seeds soaked in warm water

1/2 cup of steamed and rolled oats

1 cup of dried, mixed fruit soaked in warm water

1 teaspoon salt

dry yeast

olive oil

honey

warm water

## Preparation

1. In a large bowl, mix yeast, olive oil, honey, and warm water. Let stand for 5 minutes in a warm place, until bubbly.

2. Add flours, grains, mixed fruit, and salt and mix well by hand to form a dough. Let the dough stand in a warm place for 30 to 60 minutes until it rises to about double the size.

3. Punch down risen dough and knead for 5 minutes until the dough is smooth and rubbery, a bit like elastic.

4. Shape into three loaves.

5. Place loaves onto a greased pan. Set aside in a warm place to rise until the dough is about double in size. This takes about 45 minutes, but can take longer. If you push your finger gently into the dough and it springs back, it is ready for the oven.

6. When the dough has risen, bake at 450 degrees Fahrenheit (230 degrees Celsius) for 20 to 30 minutes.

7. Use a pot holder when removing the bread from the oven. Tap the base of the bread to check if cooked. Cooked bread will sound hollow.

8. Serve hot as a snack or toasted for breakfast.

white flour

whole-grain flour

sunflower seeds

rolled oats

salt

dried mixed fruits

# Fueling the Body with Healthy Grains, Bread, Cereal, and Pasta

The grains, bread, cereal, rice, and pasta we choose can make us feel healthy and full of energy. The best grain foods from the food pyramid are made from whole grains. They have low G.I. numbers and give us long-lasting energy.

These foods also give us lots of fiber for healthy digestion. We need to eat these foods with plenty of vegetables and fruit. We also need some meat, fish, or beans, and just a little bit of fat. This is the way to follow the healthy eating pyramid for terrific body fuel.

A sandwich made with whole-grain bread, lettuce, turkey, and sprouts makes a delicious and healthy lunch.

# Glossary

| | |
|---|---|
| **anemia** | an illness, often due to lack of iron in the diet, which causes people to become pale, tired, and weak |
| **balanced diet** | a mix of different foods that provides the right amount of nutrients for the body |
| **bolus** | a small ball of chewed food |
| **bran** | the outer skin of grains |
| **calories** | units used to measure energy |
| **cells** | microscopic structures that combine to make up all the bones, muscles, and other parts of the body |
| **chemical reactions** | processes by which substances are changed into other substances |
| **cholesterol** | a fat that is needed by the body, but which causes disease if too much is eaten |
| **diabetes** | a disease that prevents the body from producing insulin or controlling glucose |
| **digestive enzymes** | proteins that speed up the chemical reactions involved in the digestion of food |
| **endosperm** | the largest, starchy part of a grain |
| **evacuation** | removal from the body |
| **feces** | solid waste that is evacuated from the body |
| **fermented** | changed in a way that releases gases from a substance |
| **fiber** | a carbohydrate in plant foods which cannot be digested by humans |
| **germ** | the heart of a grain |
| **hormone** | a substance made in cells that helps control the body's functions |
| **immune system** | the body system that fights infections |
| **milled** | ground to break the outer husk |
| **nutrients** | substances that provide energy when eaten |
| **phytochemicals** | chemicals that occur naturally in plants |
| **rectum** | the end of the large intestine, where feces are stored before evacuation |
| **saliva** | the fluid in the mouth that helps digest food |
| **villi** | small, fingerlike bumps on the inside wall of the small intestine |
| **yeast** | a fungus that is used to make bread rise |

# Index

**A**

amylase, 9
anemia, 24

**B**

balanced diet, 4
blood, 8, 10, 11, 15, 18, 19, 21
brain, 13
bran, 17, 27

**C**

calories, 14
carbohydrates, 4, 5, 6, 7, 8, 9, 10, 11, 12, 13,
    14, 15, 17, 21, 22, 28
cells, 10, 11, 16, 18, 21, 28
cholesterol, 19, 21
celiac disease, 24, 25, 26
corn, 5, 6, 22, 25

**D**

diabetes, 11, 20
digestive enzymes, 8, 9

**E**

enriched flour, 27
essential fatty acids, 12, 13

**F**

fermentation, 9, 13, 20
fiber, 5, 12, 13, 15, 17, 19, 20, 21, 27, 28, 30
food pyramid, 4, 5, 30

**G**

glucose, 9, 10, 11, 14, 15, 19
glycemic index, 15, 16, 17

**H**

heart disease, 20

**I**

India, 6, 22
insoluble fiber, 21
insulin, 10, 11
iron, 12, 27

**K**

kilojoules, 14

**L**

large intestine, 8, 9, 13, 20
liver, 8, 13

**M**

macronutrients, 4, 8, 11, 12
micronutrients, 4, 12
millet, 6, 22, 25
minerals, 4, 7, 12, 13, 16, 17, 27, 28
mucilage fiber, 19

**N**

noodles, 7, 23
nutrients, 4, 8, 9, 10, 11, 12, 13, 20, 21, 24, 25,
    26, 27

**O**

oats, 6, 18, 21, 22, 26, 28

**P**

pancreas, 8, 9, 10
proteins, 4, 5, 12, 16, 17, 24, 27, 28

**Q**

quinoa, 25

**R**

recipes, 28–29

**S**

small intestine, 8, 9, 10, 24, 25
soluble fiber, 21
staple foods, 5, 22
stomach, 8, 9, 21

**T**

thiamine, 27
tongue, 8

**V**

vegetables, 4, 5, 6, 20, 21, 30
villi, 8, 10, 24, 25
vitamins, 4, 7, 12, 13, 16, 17, 26, 27, 28

**W**

wheat, 5, 6, 7, 18, 19, 22, 23, 24, 25, 27
whole grains, 16, 18, 19, 20, 27

**Y**

yeast, 6, 28